59372090098529   LAT

Canada

Canada

BY WIL MARA

Enchantment of the World™
Second Series

CHILDREN'S PRESS®

An Imprint of Scholastic Inc.

Frontispiece: **Banff National Park**

Consultant: Munroe Eagles, PhD, Professor and Director of Canadian Studies, University at Buffalo, Buffalo, New York
Please note: All statistics are as up-to-date as possible at the time of publication.

Book production by The Design Lab

Library of Congress Cataloging-in-Publication Data
Names: Mara, Wil, author.
Title: Canada / by Wil Mara.
Description: New York : Children's Press, an imprint of Scholastic Inc.,
  [2017] | Series: Enchantment of the world | Includes index.
Identifiers: LCCN 2016050354 | ISBN 9780531235720 (library binding)
Subjects: LCSH: Canada—Juvenile literature.
Classification: LCC F1008.2 .M294 2017 | DDC 971—dc23
LC record available at https://lccn.loc.gov/2016050354

1 2 3 4 5 6 7 8 9 10 R 27 26 25 24 23 22 21 20 19 18

Totem pole

Contents

Left to right: **Nahanni National Park Reserve, Inuit woman, Canadian Mountie, hiking, Prime Minister Justin Trudeau**

CHAPTER 1

A New Melting Pot

TWELVE-YEAR-OLD BOBBY PULLS ON HIS PARKA, throws his skates into a bag, grabs his hockey stick, and heads out the front door. It's Saturday, and Saturday means hockey at the local park.

Bobby loves all sports—basketball, baseball, soccer, lacrosse, even curling, a game in which players slide stones on the ice. But hockey's the best. His father played in a local league when he was Bobby's age, and he talks about those days like they were the happiest of his life. Bobby can understand this, as he eats, sleeps, and breathes hockey. He and his family live in southern Ontario, not far from the border his country shares with the United States. The only thing about this that bothers him is that it gets fairly warm here in the summers, which means no hockey. He could still go to one of the indoor rinks, but most of his friends won't be there—they're

Opposite: **Canada is a diverse nation. In a recent survey, Canadians reported more than two hundred different ethnic origins.**

outside playing different sports. So he just goes along and plays them, too. But the thought of hockey is never far from his mind. His greatest wish is to be a professional player one day and win the Stanley Cup, the championship trophy in the National Hockey League, the league for the best Canadian and American teams.

He gets down to the local rink, and all his friends are there. He thinks about something his dad said to him the week before—"You've got more friends of different nationalities than I ever did." Bobby has heard other people say the same thing—a lot of his friends were born in different countries, or their parents were born elsewhere. One of his friends is black. Another is Pakistani. Yet another is Jewish and was born in Israel. But his best friend, Lucas, is of French ancestry. He was born in Canada, in the province of Quebec, which has the largest French population in the country. Lucas speaks both French and English fluently, and so does Bobby. In fact, there

Kids play hockey at an outdoor ice rink in Alberta. More than a million Canadian children play hockey on a regular basis.

French is an official language in many parts of Canada.

was never a time he could remember when he couldn't speak both languages. They were taught to him in school since he was really young.

Bobby loves having friends from varied backgrounds. He likes visiting their houses and watching the different customs. Depending on their background, they sometimes dress differently, cook differently, speak differently, celebrate holidays and birthdays differently, and go to different houses of worship. Bobby finds this interesting, and despite the differences, he still thinks of his friends as essentially the same as he is. They like the same TV shows, the same junk food, the same books, the same video games, and the same sports. He thinks again about what his dad said about when he grew up, and Bobby just can't imagine growing up in that time and place.

Bobby puts his skates on as fast as he can. Once he starts zooming around the ice, he thinks that these might be some of the happiest days of his life. And he doesn't care if his friends came from Saudi Arabia or Greece or China or wherever. All he really cares about is that they are here.

More than one in five Canadians is an immigrant.

CHAPTER 2

Vast Beauty

CANADA IS A LARGE AND OFTEN COLD COUNTRY, spreading across the northernmost part of the continent of North America. Canada is the second-largest country in the world by area. At 3,855,103 square miles (9,984,670 square kilometers), it is slightly larger than the United States, the third-largest country, but much smaller than Russia, the biggest of all. Included in Canada's land are thousands of islands, most of which are located in the nation's northern reaches. A few lie within the Arctic Circle, a relatively short distance from the North Pole. Canada also boasts 151,019 miles (243,042 km) of coastline—the most of any country in the world.

Canada shares a physical border with only one other country—the United States. It meets with Alaska in the west, and twelve U.S. states along the south.

Opposite: **Mount Logan is Canada's highest point and the second-highest peak in North America. It lies in Yukon, near the border with the U.S. state of Alaska.**

The Lay of the Land

Canada is a vast country made up of a wide variety of landscapes. The largest and most prominent is the Canadian Shield, which lies in the center of the country reaching far to the north as well as to the east. The Canadian Shield is an enormous stretch of ancient rock that was scraped clean by the movement of glaciers during the last ice age. Today, the land consists of small hills and valleys covered by thin soil. There are also waterways and wetlands, plus large forested areas. Few people live in the Canadian Shield, and many who do are sustained through mining and timber activities. The Canadian Shield contains many valuable minerals, including gold, silver, and copper. Diamonds were recently discovered there.

Bales of straw sit in a field in Canada's vast interior plains.

West of the Canadian Shield, stretching all the way from the U.S. border north into the Arctic Circle, is the Canadian Interior Plains. This is mostly prairie flatland, with some areas covered by hills and forests and others providing ideal conditions for farming. Farms are common in the more southerly regions. They produce crops such as wheat, grains, and dairy products, as well as livestock.

To the west of the plains, all the way to Canada's westernmost border, is a series of mountain ranges together known as the Western Cordillera. These include the Canadian Rockies, the Columbia Mountains, and the Cariboo Mountains. These steep, rugged mountains are spectacular, with rocky slopes, narrow canyons, and crystal-clear lakes. Ice fields are common

The Canadian Rockies feature spectacular, jagged mountains.

Canada's Geographic Features

Area: 3,855,103 square miles (9,984,670 sq km)

Highest Elevation: Mount Logan, 19,551 feet (5,959 m) above sea level

Lowest Elevation: Sea level along the coast

Length of Coastline: 151,019 miles (243,042 km)

Longest River: Mackenzie River, 2,635 miles (4,241 km)

Largest Lake: Lake Superior, 31,700 square miles (82,100 sq km)

Largest Lake Entirely Within Canada: Great Bear Lake, 12,028 square miles (31,153 sq km)

Highest Recorded Temperature: 113°F (45°C), in Yellow Grass and Midale, Saskatchewan, on July 5, 1937

Lowest Recorded Temperature: –81.4°F (–63°C), in Snag, Yukon, on February 3, 1947

Greatest Annual Average Snowfall: 546 inches (1,387 cm), at Mount Fidelity, British Columbia

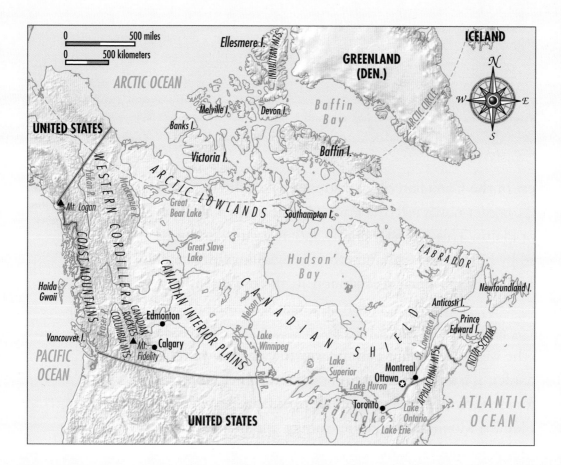

in the northern part of this region. Farther west in the cordillera are the Coast Mountains, which feature Canada's highest peaks. The nation's tallest mountain, Mount Logan, soars to 19,551 feet (5,959 meters) above sea level. Canada's Pacific Coast is renowned for its deep inlets and towering cliffs.

Canada also has two smaller mountain regions of note. The Innuitian Mountains lie in the extreme north. This area is so cold and harsh that almost no wildlife or plants survive there. Many parts of the Innuitians remain unexplored. Canada's section of the Appalachian Mountains, on the other hand,

Protecting the Land

Canada is a huge country full of magnificent scenery and wide-open spaces. Many Canadians are committed to preserving Canada's natural heritage. One way to do this is through the establishment of national parks and wildlife refuges. Today, more than 10 percent of all the land in Canada is protected, a 70 percent increase since 1995. This includes thirty-eight national parks and another eight national park reserves.

Banff, established in 1885, is Canada's oldest national park. It protects a glorious part of the Rocky Mountains. Other parks protect different kinds of landscapes. At the heart of Nahanni National Park Reserve (left) is a spectacular whitewater river and canyons in the remote Northwest Territories. Ivvavik National Park covers a vast stretch of arctic tundra. Eroded rock formations dot Mingan Archipelago National Park Reserve. And Grasslands National park preserves one of the few remaining areas of natural grasslands in the Canadian plains.

are highly populated. They begin in Canada's easternmost region of Newfoundland and Labrador and then run south through Quebec and New Brunswick into the United States. A diverse array of plants and animals lives in the Canadian Appalachians, and many areas are ideal for farming.

Canada's Arctic Lowlands are located in the northern part of the country. The largest section is sandwiched between the Canadian Shield and the southern part of Hudson Bay, a sea in northeastern Canada that opens onto both the Atlantic and

Glaciers float on the Arctic waters in northern Canada.

the Arctic Oceans. The rest of the lowlands lay among scattered islands within the Arctic Circle. The Arctic Lowlands are characterized by extreme cold and dryness, with poor soil that makes farming impossible. The lowlands do have abundant mineral deposits, however, as well as natural gas and oil.

The other major Canadian region is the Great Lakes–St. Lawrence Lowlands. The region spreads out from the Great Lakes that Canada shares with the United States. These lowlands were once highly forested, but logging, farming, towns, and cities have dramatically reduced the amount of forests.

Big Cities

Canada has many cities with populations of at least half a million. With more than 2.7 million residents, Toronto is the most populous city in Canada, and the fourth largest in all of North America. It is also the capital city of the province of Ontario and sits on the shores of Lake Ontario, one of the Great Lakes. Toronto was established in 1793 and became an important industrial and trading center. In the twentieth century, the city grew rapidly, and today it is the commercial heart of the country. The city is filled with skyscrapers and boasts the tallest structure in the Western Hemisphere,

the CN Tower (left), which is 1,815 feet (553 m) tall. Toronto is considered one of the world's most pleasant cities in which to live. It is known for efficient public transportation, clean streets, and affordable prices. It is also one of the most culturally diverse cities in the world. More than half the city's residents were born in another country, and they speak about two hundred languages.

Montreal (above), Canada's second-largest city, has more than 1.7 million residents, almost all of whom are fluent in the French language. The city gets its name from the mountain around which it was built, Mont Royal. Montreal was founded by French colonists in the 1600s, and it still has some buildings that date back to that era. Montreal also has an underground city with a network of tunnels that links stores, restaurants, museums, schools, and other sites, so that pedestrians can avoid going outside, especially in the frigid winter.

When it comes to western Canada, no city beats Calgary (above). It has about 1.2 million residents. Calgary is located where the prairie meets the Rockies. Calgary is a young city, founded in 1875, but it quickly became an economic powerhouse, first as part of the cattle industry and later as the center of Canada's oil industry. In 1988, it became the first Canadian city to host the Winter Olympics. Today, the city is known for having great cultural diversity, with more than 140 different languages spoken there.

Canada's fourth-largest city is its capital, Ottawa, while its fifth largest is Edmonton. With more than 900,000 people in the city and another 1.2 million in the metro area, Edmonton is the most northerly city in North America with more than a million residents. The city is located on Canada's fertile plains, about 200 miles (300 km) north of Calgary. Like Calgary,

Edmonton plays a significant role in Canada's oil industry. The city also boasts the largest mall in all of North America—the West Edmonton Mall (below), the site of more than eight hundred shops and enough parking for more than twenty thousand cars.

Climate

Many people think of Canada as icy because it is located in the north, but the truth is that much of the country has four distinct seasons. Summers can be hot and humid in the more southerly areas, where most of the people live, while spring and autumn are usually pleasant, with people needing only a light jacket. In many places, however, winter can be bitterly cold. The frigid winds, blowing snow, and days with little sun-

Pedestrians make their way through a snowstorm in Toronto. In many parts of Canada, the ground is covered with snow from mid-autumn until spring.

Light rain is frequent in British Columbia, which helps maintain the region's rich, lush forests.

light can make winter challenging, although most Canadians know how to make do.

The amounts of rain and snow that fall varies tremendously across Canada. The coastal forests of British Columbia, for example, are lush, receiving more than 100 inches (250 centimeters) a year. Rainfall is also abundant in the Great Lakes region. The snowiest regions of the country are in the mountains of the West. The interior plains and Arctic regions, although extremely cold, receive little rain and snow because the air there is so dry.

A Disappointment at First

Canada's longest waterway is the Mackenzie River, whose name came from the Scottish explorer Alexander Mackenzie. Mackenzie went down the river in 1789 with the hope that it would take him to the Pacific Ocean. It brought him to the Arctic Ocean instead, and thus he originally named it Disappointment River. Snaking 2,635 miles (4,241 km), the Mackenzie ranks as the eleventh-longest river in the world. Its source is Great Slave Lake, located in the Yukon region of the Northwest Territories, and it moves northwest toward the Arctic. The Mackenzie and its tributaries drain much of the land in northwestern Canada.

Waterways

Canada is a land rich in water. About 7 percent of the world's supply of accessible fresh water comes from Canadian rivers

Canada's many wetlands are vital habitats for a variety of wildlife.

and lakes. Nearly a quarter of the world's wetlands are found within its borders, and there are literally millions of Canadian lakes. Canada is also home to more glaciers than any other place except Greenland and Antarctica.

Canada's largest lakes are the Great Lakes. Four of the five Great Lakes serve as part of the border between Canada and the United States. Other major lakes include Great Bear Lake and Great Slave Lake, both in Canada's northern stretches. Canada's longest river, the Mackenzie, begins in Great Slave Lake and drains into the Arctic Ocean in the north. Other major rivers include the St. Lawrence, in southeastern Canada, and the Fraser and the Yukon in the west.

The movement of glaciers helped sculpt the rocky shoreline along Lake Huron.

CHAPTER 3

Living Things

SINCE CANADA COVERS SUCH A VAST AREA, IT HAS
a tremendous amount of diversity. There are arctic areas
where giant sheets of ice cover vast expanses of rock, and little
life can be found. But there are also plains, prairies, wetlands,
lakes, forests, and even rain forests. Within each of these eco-
logical niches thrives an incredible array of living things.

Animal Life

Wildlife abounds in Canada. The forests are filled with a wide
variety of mammals, ranging from black bears and wolves to
rabbits and raccoons. Bighorn sheep, mountain goats, and elk
make their homes in the western mountains.

One of the animals most associated with Canada is the
moose. The largest member of the deer family, it stands about

Moose eat only plants. They often eat more than 50 pounds (23 kilograms) of food a day.

6 feet (1.8 m) high at the shoulder. Moose are found throughout Canada and in parts of the northern United States, as well as in Russia and northern Europe. They live mostly in forested areas, where they survive on a diet of leaves, twigs, fruit, and other plant parts. Male moose have striking branch-like antlers that are covered with a soft, velvety material. The size of the antlers depends on the moose's age and diet. Moose use their antlers to fend off predators or to fight other moose when competing for a mate.

Canada's plains are home to many small animals, such as squirrels, gophers, and mice. The largest mammals that live on the plains are mule deer and pronghorn antelope. Pronghorns are relatively small, standing only about 3 feet (1 m) tall, but they are the fastest land mammal in the Americas. They can reach speeds of 55 miles per hour (89 kph).

Farther north is the region known as tundra. This is an area that is so cold that trees do not grow. Fewer types of animals live in tundra regions. In Canada, the tundra is home to mammals such as arctic foxes, arctic hares, and caribou.

Northern Canada is tundra, where no trees grow and where the soil underground is frozen year-round.

Probably the best-known animal in the Canadian tundra is the polar bear. Polar bears live in icy areas and are excellent swimmers, frequently diving into the frigid seawater. Their heavy coats of both fur and fatty tissue, sometimes 4 inches (10 cm) thick, help them withstand subfreezing temperatures. A polar bear's primary diet is seals, which it will catch by waiting at holes in the ice until one surfaces for air. When seals are not available, polar bears will eat a variety of other mammals, birds, fish, and eggs, and even some plant matter.

A polar bear cub gets a ride from its mother. The white coat of polar bears tends to yellow as they age.

National Animal

Canada's national animal is the beaver. It was chosen because beavers were at the heart of the fur trade, which was vital to the European development of Canada. Beavers are found throughout the nation.

A beaver grows about 3.5 feet (1 m) long, including its paddle-shaped tail. They are built for life in the water, with webbed hind feet and two layers of fur—a short, fine inner layer and a heavier outer layer—which can be made waterproof by an oily substance it produces in its scent glands.

The beaver is a remarkable animal in that it remakes its habitat to suit its own needs. Beavers topple trees to the ground by gnawing on them with their long front teeth. They use these trees, along with other sticks, branches, rocks, and grass, to build dams across streams. The dams create large ponds where the beavers build a lodge, their home, out of sticks and logs.

A beaver lodge has an underwater entrance, which helps protect the creatures from predators. If a beaver simply built its lodge along a stream, it would not have the best protection and the swift-moving water might wash it away.

Trees are important to beavers not only as a source of lumber but also as part of their diet. The animals eat tree bark and the softer tissue just underneath it.

Beavers do not group together socially like some animals. They pick a mate for life and have a litter of about three or four young, called kits, once per year. The young remain with the parents for around two years before moving off to build their own lodges in a nearby area.

More than 450 bird species live in Canada. Great snowy owls live in the tundra. Hawks, eagles, and other birds of prey soar high above the land. The forests are filled with jays and finches and crows. Warblers and many other kinds of songbirds migrate to Canada's forests to breed, while ducks, geese, and loons build nests along lakeshores.

One of the most abundant birds in Canada is the Canada goose. These hardy animals can thrive in a variety of habitats, including grasslands, forests, mountains, prairies, farmland,

A great gray owl snatches prey from beneath the snow in Manitoba. The great gray is the world's largest owl species.

and even suburbs and cities. Many seek out tundra regions during breeding season and then migrate to warmer southern areas when winter comes. Canada geese choose a mate when they reach about two years of age, and they stay with that mate for life. A female goose lays between two and ten eggs at a time. Both the male and female protect the eggs.

Canada geese swim in a pond in Vancouver, British Columbia. They live throughout Canada, often gathering in large flocks.

Plant Life

More than 40 percent of the land in Canada is covered by forest. In fact, Canada is home to about 10 percent of all the forest cover on the planet.

White birch trees thrive in Canada's cool climate.

The variety of trees native to Canada is remarkable. There are firs, pines, spruces, redwoods, alders, birches, ashes, oaks, and many more. Hardwoods such as maples and oaks are prominent in the Great Lakes region, while conifers, or cone-bearing trees, are found in the north. Among the most common trees in the northern forests are spruce, birch, and balsam fir. In the moist forests of British Columbia, Douglas fir, western hemlock, and red cedar are common.

The interior plains were once covered with short grasses, but much of that land has now been turned into farms. Ferns abound in the damp western forests, while wild blueberries grow in clearings and fields in the Atlantic region.

Symbol of the Nation

The national tree is the maple, and the leaf of the maple tree has become a symbol for Canada. For example, Canada's flag features a red maple leaf. Maples have importance to the nation beyond their symbolism. Canadian maple syrup is considered among the best in the world and plays an important role in the economy. Maple timber is particularly durable and therefore ideal in the manufacture of everything from furniture to baseball bats and bowling pins.

The nation's most widespread shrub is the Canada buffaloberry. It is noted mostly for its hardiness and its small, bright-red berries, which are often called soapberries because

A black bear in Yukon forages for Canada buffaloberries.

they contain a substance that gets sudsy in water. These have been harvested by Canadians for centuries. They are not usually eaten plain, as they have a harsh, bitter flavor. They are sometimes mixed with other, sweeter berries to balance out their sourness. More often, they are used in a type of ice cream called Sxusem (pronounced (s-KHU-sum).

Many people assume that the coldest regions of the country have little in the way of plants. But this is not the case.

Thick moss covers the ground and fallen trees in Haida Gwaii, an island off the coast of British Columbia.

Even in some of the most frigid regions, there is life. Mosses, for example, are plentiful in such areas. Moss is a tiny, flowerless plant that usually grows in thick mats. It thrives in locations that are damp and have little light. Most moss species grow no more than 1 or 2 inches (2.5 or 5 cm) tall.

Similarly hardy are liverworts, which also thrive in moist places with minimal sunlight. They can cover broad areas in a dense, colorful carpet. Some liverworts produce leaves and flowers. They are commonly found on rocky surfaces, looking more like squishy blobs than their sleek and velvety moss relatives.

Another category of living things found in Canada is fungi. These are not plants, and they are not animals. Mold, for example, is a form of fungus, as are mushrooms. Fungi are hardy and highly adaptable, and as such, scientists believe there are literally millions of species found in every environment around the world.

Fly agaric mushrooms are one of the many colorful mushroom species that grow in Canada.

CHAPTER 4

Past and Present

THE EARLIEST PEOPLES BELIEVED TO HAVE INHABITED the area known today as Canada arrived at least twelve thousand years ago. At the time, the climate was colder than it is today, and much of the world's water was frozen into ice. This made the sea level lower and exposed a strip of land between what are now Russia and the U.S. state of Alaska. This enabled people from Asia to walk to North America in their search for warmer climates and greater food supplies.

Opposite: **A Cree doll. The Cree were one of many indigenous groups that lived on the Interior Plains.**

The First Canadians

Over time, the people spread out across the continent. By two thousand years ago, a group of widely dispersed yet similar cultures had developed in the Great Lakes region and much farther south, in what is now the United States. Together, these people are known as the Hopewell culture. These societies forged relationships with their neighbors and began to trade goods. The Hopewell network produced some

Indigenous Groups, 1500

of the earliest surviving examples of Canadian artwork, pottery, and jewelry, most made of wood, stone, shells, and clay, as well as animal parts like teeth and bone. Precious metals such as copper and silver were also used. By about 500 CE, the Hopewell culture had declined.

In the following centuries, a wide variety of indigenous, or native, cultures developed throughout what would become Canada. In the forests of the east were a large number of groups who spoke related Algonquian languages. Also numerous were the Iroquois people, who lived farther west. Both these groups lived in longhouses in the summer. Longhouses varied widely in length, with some reaching

Potlatches

The indigenous people of Canada belonged to dozens of ethnic groups that developed vastly different cultures. For example, ethnic groups on the Pacific coast, known as the Northwest Coast peoples, lived in one place year-round, and they developed complex ceremonies. One ceremony common to many Northwest Coast groups is the potlatch. During a potlatch, a prominent person would hold a great feast, which included ceremonial dancing, often by people wearing elaborate masks. And then the person holding the potlatch would give valuable gifts to everyone who attended. In part, potlatches were a way for the Northwest Coast peoples to cement their social status. The more powerful a person was, the larger the potlatch would be.

more than 300 feet (90 m) long. Each longhouse housed several families. The people hunted, fished, and tended gardens where they grew corn and other crops. On the plains were groups such as the Blackfeet and Kainai. The plains people frequently moved, following the herds of bison that were their main food source. On the Pacific coast were a number of peoples such as the Salishan and Tsimshian, who survived on fishing and the bounty they could find in the damp forests of the region. Farther north in the Arctic, the Inuits were skilled fishers and hunters.

Europeans Arrive

The European colonization of North America had a profound impact on the indigenous people who already lived there. The first Europeans to arrive in what is now Canada were Norwegian sailors, often called Vikings, who reached Newfoundland, in northeastern Canada, around the year 1000. Their settlements did not endure, however.

A few centuries later, John Cabot, an Italian sailing for Great Britain, reached the coast of Newfoundland. He stayed just long enough to plant a few flags and

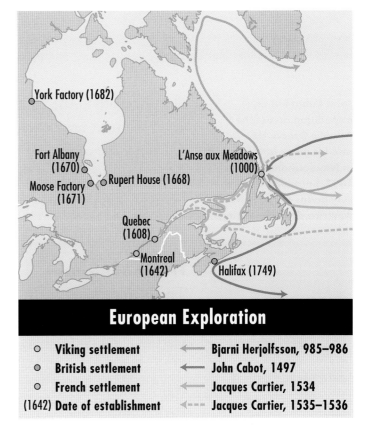

York Factory (1682)

Fort Albany (1670)

Moose Factory (1671)

Rupert House (1668)

L'Anse aux Meadows (1000)

Quebec (1608)

Montreal (1642)

Halifax (1749)

European Exploration

○ Viking settlement	← Bjarni Herjolfsson, 985–986
◉ British settlement	← John Cabot, 1497
○ French settlement	← Jacques Cartier, 1534
(1642) Date of establishment	←--- Jacques Cartier, 1535–1536

John Cabot led an expedition across the Atlantic Ocean. He and his party landed in Newfoundland in 1497, becoming the first Europeans to reach North America since the Vikings.

claim the site in the name of King Henry VII before sailing off. Over the next few decades, explorers from other nations would sail along the coast, and both Spain and Portugal claimed areas at one time or another. But there was no meaningful interaction between Europeans and native North Americans until about the mid-1500s.

French Settlement

The French were the first Europeans to commit to the idea of building a society in what is now Canada. In 1534, Jacques Cartier led a party along the Atlantic coast and into the Gulf of St. Lawrence. In Quebec, he planted a cross, claiming the region for France. He returned the following year and explored farther down the St. Lawrence River. Cartier had hoped to find precious minerals in the area, but was unsuccessful. The region was, however, rich in wildlife. Other explorers ventured into the area, but it wasn't until the 1600s that any permanent settlements were established.

In 1603, the French king gave merchant Pierre du Gua, sieur de Monts a monopoly on the fur trade. It was the fur of animals, particularly beavers, that would drive the economy of the young French colony. The pelts of beavers and other animals were used to make hats, coats, and other goods. Samuel de Champlain, one of du Gua's men, attempted to establish a settlement along the coast in 1604. This effort failed, but in 1608, Champlain established Quebec City, the first permanent European settlement in Canada. By this time, the explorers had mapped out a colony they called New France.

Into the Woods

The fur trade was the driving force behind the early French settlement of Canada, and central to the fur trade were people known as *coureurs de bois*, "runners of the woods." These were traders who went into the woods to trade with the indigenous people. They lived among the native people and learned their languages, and the ways of the woods. They learned to travel by canoe and live off the land. They also ended up exploring much of the Great Lakes region. By the late 1600s, the coureurs were replaced by voyageurs, who were representatives of fur-trading companies. But the coureurs remained part of Canadian mythology, romanticized as brave, independent woodsmen.

In the 1600s, the English also began sending representatives to colonize the area and benefit from its abundance of natural resources. The Scots jumped into the mix, claiming a region that would become known as Nova Scotia (Latin for "New Scotland").

While the English and the Scottish concentrated their colonial efforts mostly in coastal areas, the French focused on expanding westward. Their power in these interior areas raised tensions not only with other Europeans but also with the native peoples of the region. From the mid-1600s to the mid-1700s, many wars erupted between France and England, with each aided by Native American allies. The most notable of these battles was a series of conflicts known as the French and Indian Wars, fought between 1688 and 1763. By the end of the final French and Indian War, French holdings in what is now Canada had dramatically declined. The French had ceded much of their territory to the English.

The Money Pit

A favorite Canadian myth concerns Oak Island, a small island off the southern shore of Nova Scotia, one of more than 350 islands in the area. What makes Oak Island unique are the stories of buried treasure there that have inspired hundreds of expeditions. One part of the island is known as the Money Pit. In the 1800s, treasure seekers dug around the site in search of riches supposedly buried by the pirate Captain Kidd two hundred years earlier. People discovered several depressions in the earth. When these were excavated, they revealed layers of timber and stone. The treasure seekers believed that these had been put there by Kidd or his crew to protect the treasure. Over the years, many people dug in the area to see if they could find the riches. Eventually, the holes they dug reached all the way down to the water table. Other depressions have been discovered, and even today some people believe a vast fortune lies waiting for them underground. As of yet, however, not a single piece of pirate's gold or silver has been found.

Under British Rule

At the conclusion of the French and Indian Wars in 1763, and for roughly the next one hundred years, the British ruled Canada. Although some French colonists were expelled from the area, the British mostly honored already established French traditions. In 1774, the British Parliament passed the Quebec Act, which preserved French ways in Quebec. Under this act, the Roman Catholic religion was allowed, and Catholics in Quebec could hold office. The act also preserved the French system of civil law.

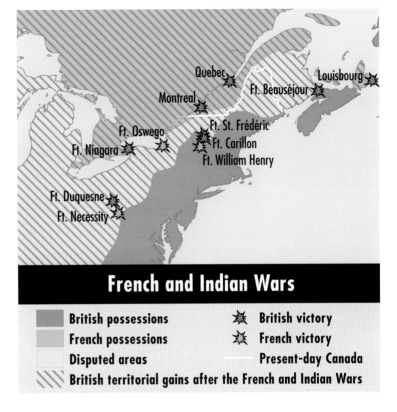

French and Indian Wars

British possessions	British victory
French possessions	French victory
Disputed areas	Present-day Canada
British territorial gains after the French and Indian Wars	

Under British rule, the fur trade continued to drive the Canadian economy. Many indigenous people were hired to trap beavers and other animals. When the fur trade began to decline in the 1830s, largely because of the changing fashion tastes in Europe, the timber trade became Canada's economic engine. Timber was in great demand in England, because most of the timber supply there had been exhausted in the previous centuries.

Conflicts to the South

In 1775, the colonies to the south of Canada rose up against the British in the American Revolution. Some of the battles spilled over into southeastern Canada, particularly Quebec.

General John Burgoyne (right), a British officer, recruited Native Americans as well as Loyalists to fight against the rebelling American colonists during the American Revolution.

Canadians were divided on the issue of American independence, but the American colonists fighting for independence found many sympathizers in places where French Canadians remembered their own losses to the British. Canada also served as a place of refuge for tens of thousands of American colonists who remained loyal to the British crown and felt unwelcome in the newly formed United States. This immigrant population included a small number of black former slaves who fought for the British cause and were freed when the war ended.

The other major British conflict fought partly on Canadian land was the War of 1812. This resulted from rising tensions between Great Britain and the United States over a range of issues, including Britain's attempts to block U.S. expansion to the West and its ongoing trade relationship with France. U.S. forces attempted to capture areas in British-ruled Canada, mostly in the Great Lakes region, but the British and their Native American allies held them off. Battles continued with neither side achieving victory, and the war finally ended in 1815.

British and American ships battle in Lake Erie during the War of 1812.

Toward Independence

In the following decades, many of the same tensions that had caused the American colonists to seek independence began to arise among the Canadian people. Canadians complained about unfair governance, in which ordinary citizens felt disregarded or exploited in order to line the pockets of the wealthy. Since many of the wealthy had a strong influence in government—or were part of the government—they felt little desire to change the situation. As reformists began to gain power, some people rose up in the Rebellions of 1837 and 1838, but the British defeated them.

During the 1837 uprising, some rebels used a ship named the *Caroline*. The Canadian forces attacked the ship while it was in the Niagara River, on the border between the United States and Canada, set it ablaze, and let it drift over Niagara Falls.

By the 1840s, it became clear that a more balanced system of representative government was needed, and by the mid-1860s, the British were becoming concerned that the United States would take advantage of the discord within Canada and try to claim areas of the country for itself. They believed that a united set of Canadian colonies was the best way to avert this, so in July 1867, a confederation called the Dominion of Canada was formed.

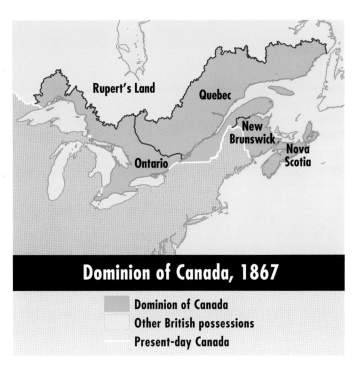

Dominion of Canada, 1867

Dominion of Canada
Other British possessions
Present-day Canada

On Their Own

The Dominion of Canada included four provinces—Ontario, Quebec, Nova Scotia, and New Brunswick. Canada's new governing system was similar to that of the United States, except Canada continued to recognize the British monarch as its head of state, rather than having a president. Many Canadians believed that maintaining their connection with the British monarchy would inspire a sense of continuity and national identity. The British also retained control of foreign policy. In addition, Canada's constitutional document was a law passed by the British.

In the years that followed the formation of the Dominion of Canada, the four provinces elected representatives to send

Train tracks were laid across Canada in the mid-1800s. In some places, the tracks had to cross deep canyons.

to their newly formed parliament. In 1867, they appointed their first prime minister, Sir John A. Macdonald, who had been a driving force in the creation of the confederation. In the 1870s, other areas joined the confederation, including Manitoba, the Northwest Territories, British Columbia, and Prince Edward Island. The Yukon Territory, Saskatchewan, and Alberta joined around the start of the twentieth century. Newfoundland and Labrador joined later, in 1949, and Nunavut in 1999.

A New Age

By the dawn of the twentieth century, Canada had developed a solid infrastructure. Railroad tracks ran all the way across the country. The Royal Canadian Mounted Police had been formed to guard the nation's southern border against possible interference from the United States. Large numbers of immigrants arrived from the British Isles and northern Europe, many drawn by a booming agricultural industry. People explored remote areas and discovered vast natural resources. In the late 1890s, a hundred thousand prospectors flooded into the Yukon during the Klondike Gold Rush, hoping to make their fortune. Only a few hundred became rich, however, and most had left by 1900.

A long line of prospectors heads for the Klondike gold fields in 1898.

One of the most significant events for Canada in the early twentieth century was its involvement in World War I. The war began in 1914, and Canadians joined the British and other allies in their fight against Germany and the Central powers. Prior to this, Canada had a small standing army that was tasked primarily with protecting Canada's borders.

Once the war began, however, Canada quickly enlarged its army, drafting more than half a million people into active duty. Many Canadians saw this involvement in the war as another step in their country developing its own identity. In the war's early stages, many Canadian units had British leaders. In time, however, Canada produced its own military commanders. By the war's end in 1918, about 61,000 Canadian soldiers had died and another 200,000 were wounded out of a

Fiction Comes to Life

Located in Cavendish within the Prince Edward Island National Park, the former working farm known as Green Gables is among Canada's most popular tourist destinations. It also has an alternate name—the Green Gables Heritage Place. Thousands of people come from around the world to visit the site that inspired the setting for L. M. Montgomery's beloved tales found in *Anne of Green Gables*, first published in 1908. In addition to the Green Gables house itself, there are several museums where visitors can learn more about Anne and her creator. There is also a popular musical version of the story featured every summer at the local Charlottetown Festival.

total of 620,000 who served overseas. In spite of these painful losses, the wartime experience gave Canada greater status and respect around the world.

Canada suffered tremendous hardship in the Great Depression, which struck in 1929 and continued through much of the following decade. Businesses closed, banks failed, and the unemployment rate rose until one out of every four Canadians was jobless. Many people had to rely on government help for the first time in their lives. Rural areas were particularly hard hit.

With the outbreak of World War II, Canada once again found itself pulled into a global conflict. Canada sided with the Allies, led by Great Britain, the United States, and the

Unemployed Canadians head to Ottawa in 1935 in a protest march. At the height of the Great Depression, 30 percent of the labor force in Canada was out of work.

Tens of thousands of German soldiers were sent to prisoner of war camps in Canada during World War II. The two largest camps, which each held more than twelve thousand prisoners, were in Alberta.

Soviet Union, in their fight against the Axis powers, led by Germany and Japan. Canada was significantly involved in the war, taking part in major Allied invasions of Europe and fending off German naval attacks along the Atlantic coast. More than one million Canadians served in World War II; about forty-five thousand were killed, and another fifty-five thousand were wounded.

Because of Canada's great military value, the United States built many roads, railways, and bases there during the war. The two nations were fighting common enemies, and their cooperation drew them closer together. The war benefited Canada's economy, as wartime needs led to a surge in manufacturing. This economic boom ended the Great Depression and returned Canada to prosperity.

After the War

Following World War II, Canada continued to strengthen its ties with the United States while increasing its profile on the world stage. It helped found the North Atlantic Treaty Organization (NATO), a military alliance among Canada, the United States, and many European nations. And it participated in peacekeeping activities during the Suez Crisis, a nine-day conflict in Egypt in November 1956. Future Canadian prime minister Lester Pearson received the Nobel Peace Prize for his work in ending the crisis.

A woman works in an arms factory in Canada during World War II. Hundreds of thousands of Canadian women worked in military factories during the war.

The two decades after World War II were a time of prosperity for Canada. Manufacturing and mining expanded, and suburbs grew up around cities. Freeways were built, and the population grew. Canada also experienced large-scale immigration after the war. Many of the newcomers came from countries in southern Europe, such as Italy and Greece.

In the 1960s, Canada experienced a period of social upheaval. The tensions between French- and English-speaking citizens heated up in Quebec. Some Quebecois wanted the province to separate from the rest of Canada. In 1968, a

German and Italian immigrants work on a railroad in Canada. Many of the workers who laid new track in Canada in the 1950s were immigrants.

Quebecois politician named Pierre Trudeau became prime minister. Trudeau did not want Quebec to separate from the rest of Canada, but he did support French culture in Quebec. In 1969, the Official Languages Act was passed giving French and English equal status as official languages, and giving Canadians the right to interact with the government in whichever language they preferred.

Some people in Quebec continued to argue for independence, and they began using violence to achieve their goal. The boiling point was reached in 1970 with the October Crisis. This included the kidnap and murder of a cabinet minister named Pierre Laporte and a British diplomat named James Cross by the radical organization Front de Libération du Québec (FLQ), which supported independence for Quebec. Troops were sent into Quebec and hundreds of people were arrested.

Young people in Montreal in 1970 demonstrate in support of an independent Quebec.

Pierre Trudeau

Pierre Trudeau was the dominant figure in Canadian political life from the late 1960s through the early 1980s. He was born in Montreal in 1919, the son of a successful French-Canadian businessman. Young Trudeau was a brilliant student who studied law, politics, and economics at the University of Montreal and at Harvard University in Massachusetts, as well as in Paris and London. He worked as a law professor before joining the government and becoming the minister of justice. Trudeau became prime minister in 1968, a position he held for most of the next fifteen years. With a powerful combination of charisma, immense intellect, and a masterful sense of the media, he became a popular leader. Trudeau worked to improve relations between English and French Canadians, and to increase government support for bilingualism and multiculturalism. He also worked to strengthen Canada's relations with other countries around the world.

In 1982, Canada achieved full independence from Great Britain with the Constitution Act. At the same time, the Canadian Charter of Rights and Freedoms was passed, which guarantees people basic rights such as freedom of religion, the right to free expression, and the right to vote.

Despite the changes in Canada, the issue of Quebec's independence continued to swirl. In 1995, the people of Quebec voted on a referendum on whether to remain part of Canada. The vote was very close, but they voted against independence. In the years since, support for an independent Quebec has faded.

To the Present

In recent years, Canada has continued to enhance its ties with the United States. In 1994, Canada, the United States, and Mexico signed the North American Free Trade Agreement, eliminating many trade barriers between the nations, such as taxes on some goods. Canada and the United States have also worked together on issues such as border security.

In 2005, Canada took a leap forward socially when it became the first nation in the Americas to legalize same-sex marriage.

By 2015, the economy was in decline. Conservative Party leaders had been in charge for nearly a decade, and Canadians voted for a change. The Liberal Party gained control of the federal government, and Justin Trudeau, the eldest son of Pierre Trudeau, became prime minister. Trudeau is committed to welcoming immigrants and supporting Canadian diversity, which, over time, has become central to Canadian identity.

Prime Minister Justin Trudeau (center) is a strong advocate for Canadian diversity.

CHAPTER 5

Running the Country

CANADA'S GOVERNMENT IS SIMILAR IN MANY WAYS to that of the United States, yet there are significant differences. One of the most important parallels is that both governments are democracies guided by principles set forth in a constitution. In democracies, the people decide through elections who will represent them in the government.

One of the differences is that the U.S. head of state is the president, whereas in Canada it is the monarch of England, Queen Elizabeth II. The British monarch has little actual power in Canada, however. Her role is primarily ceremonial, and most of her duties are carried out by the governor general, her representative in Canada.

Opposite: **The building where the Canadian Parliament meets dates to the early twentieth century.**

National Flag

Canada's national flag consists of two vertical bars of red on either side and a wider white field between them, with a red maple leaf in the center. Red and white have been Canada's official colors since King George V handed down the proclamation of the Royal Arms of Canada in 1921. The idea for the maple leaf was first suggested by George Stanley, a professor at the Royal Military College in Kingston, in 1964. He felt this simple design could be seen easily from a distance. The symbol of the leaf itself has been in use by Canada since the eighteenth century.

Legislative Branch

Canada's legislative body, or parliament, has two parts. The House of Commons has 338 members who are elected by the people from districts. The House of Commons is the more powerful of the two parts of parliament.

The other half of Canada's parliament is the Senate, which has 105 members. Twenty-four members represent each of Canada's four major regions—the Maritime Provinces (along the Atlantic coast), Ontario, Quebec, and the Western Provinces. The other parts of Canada are represented by the remaining nine senators. Members of the Senate are appointed officially by the governor general, although the choices are actually made by the prime minister, the head of the government. The Senate is much less powerful than the House of Commons. It can slow down legislation, but it cannot veto bills.

National Government of Canada

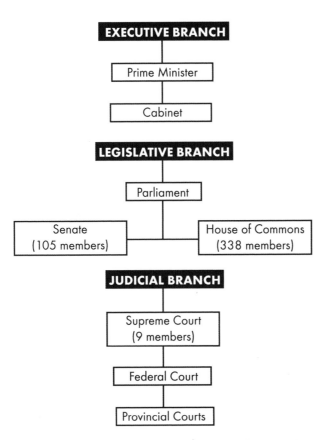

EXECUTIVE BRANCH

Prime Minister

Cabinet

LEGISLATIVE BRANCH

Parliament

Senate
(105 members)

House of Commons
(338 members)

JUDICIAL BRANCH

Supreme Court
(9 members)

Federal Court

Provincial Courts

Executive Branch

Canada's executive branch is not headed by a president, the way the U.S. executive branch is. Rather, it is headed by a prime minister, who is aided by a cabinet made up of politicians called ministers. The cabinet has no set number of members; in recent times, there have been about three dozen. Each minister is responsible for a different area of government concern, such as health, foreign affairs, and transportation.

Most cabinet members are experienced government figures, including members of parliament, military figures, or judges. They are chosen by the prime minister.

The prime minister is usually the leader of the political party that holds the majority of seats in the House of Commons. The prime minister is the most important politician in Canada and the face of the Canadian government around the world. Most legislation is introduced by the prime minister's cabinet, and bills usually have strong support from their party members in the House of Commons. The party leaders generally tell their party members how to vote.

The Canadian Parliament meets in Ottawa in a grand set of buildings called the Centre Block.

Justin Trudeau

In 2015, Justin Trudeau, the leader of the Liberal Party, became the prime minister of Canada. Trudeau, the son of longtime Canadian prime minister Pierre Trudeau, grew up while his father was in office. He first came to public prominence with the moving remarks he gave at his father's funeral in 2000.

Trudeau worked as a teacher and as an advocate for environmental and other issues before entering politics. He ran for parliament for the first time in 2008, winning a seat from a district in Montreal. With his youth and charisma, his political power grew quickly. He became the leader of the Liberal Party in 2013, and two years later he became the second-youngest prime minister in Canadian history. As prime minister, he has continued to work to protect the environment and strengthen Canada's growing diversity.

Because the prime minister and the majority of members of parliament are from the same party, it is much easier for a party platform to get passed there than in the United States. This means that at the end of a term, Canadian voters can evaluate their representatives' success and decide whether to vote them in again.

The prime minister normally governs as long as a majority of members of parliament support the legislation of his or her government. If a government fails to attract a majority of votes from members of the House of Commons for an important piece of legislation, the House of Commons can pass a vote of "no confidence," and a new election will often be called. So while a government can last as long as five years, it can also be voted out of office after a much shorter time.

Canada's capital city, Ottawa, is its fourth-largest city, with a population of about 900,000. It is located in the southeastern tip of the province of Ontario. Ottawa's original name was Bytown, which honored Lieutenant Colonel John By, the engineer who supervised construction of the Rideau Canal. The city was given the name Ottawa in 1855, after the Algonquian word *adawe*, meaning "to trade." In 1857, it was named Canada's capital.

Ottawa is a clean, attractive city that draws many kinds of people. About half the population is under the age of thirty-five. The city is home to many immigrants, and about one in every four residents was born outside the country. It also boasts Canada's most educated population, as it is home to more people with

doctorates—the highest degree a person can receive—than any other Canadian city. Many people who live in the city work for the government. Many technology companies and hospitals are also located there. The city is filled with museums, including the National Gallery of Canada, the Canadian Museum of History, and the Canadian Museum of Nature.

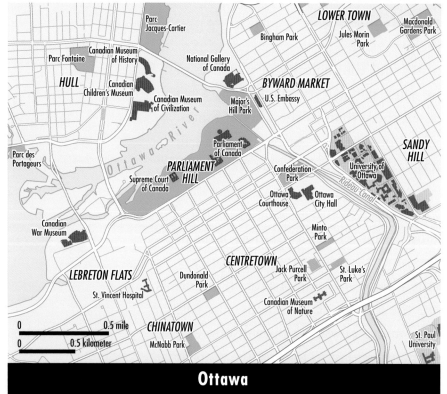

Ottawa

The Judicial Branch

The Supreme Court of Canada is the highest court in the nation. It has nine judges, all appointed by the governor general on the prime minister's advice. It primarily reviews decisions made by lower courts. Both federal (national) and provincial courts are below the Supreme Court. Each system has both trial courts and appeals courts. Cases start in the trial courts, can be reviewed in appeals courts, and then can be appealed again to the Supreme Court.

Justices of the Canadian Supreme Court wear special robes during the welcome ceremony at the beginning of each term.

Regional Government

Canada is divided into provinces and territories, rather than states like in the United States. The nation has ten provinces—Alberta, British Columbia, Manitoba, New Brunswick, Newfoundland and Labrador, Nova Scotia, Ontario, Prince Edward Island, Quebec, and Saskatchewan. It also has three territories—Northwest Territories, Nunavut, and the Yukon—which are much less populated than

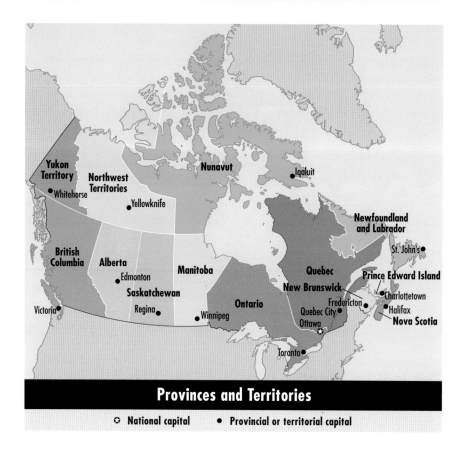

Provinces and Territories

○ National capital   • Provincial or territorial capital

the provinces. Each province or territory has its own capital city, legislature, judicial system, and official language.

The person who acts on the queen's behalf in each province is called the lieutenant governor. The governor general appoints this person on the advice of the prime minister. A similar position in the territories is known as a commissioner.

Because Canada has significant cultural and regional differences, power is divided between national and provincial governments. The provinces have more power than states do in the United States. In fact, Canada has developed into one of the most decentralized federal systems in the world. In part, this is because of Quebec's desire to protect the status of the French language and culture in Canada.

National Anthem

The words to "O Canada" were written in the early 1900s, but the song was not officially adopted as Canada's national anthem until 1980. The anthem has official English lyrics, official French lyrics, and a version that mixes the two.

English lyrics

O Canada! Our home and native land!
True patriot love in all thy sons command.
With glowing hearts we see thee rise,
The True North strong and free!
From far and wide,
O Canada, we stand on guard for thee.
God keep our land glorious and free!
O Canada, we stand on guard for thee.
O Canada, we stand on guard for thee.

French lyrics

O Canada! Terre de nos aïeux,
Ton front est ceint de fleurons glorieux!
Car ton bras sait porter l'épée,
Il sait porter la croix!
Ton histoire est une épopée
Des plus brillants exploits.
Et ta valeur, de foi trempée,
Protégera nos foyers et nos droits.
Protégera nos foyers et nos droits.

Bilingual lyrics

O Canada! Our home and native land!
True patriot love in all thy sons command,
Car ton bras sait porter l'épée,
Il sait porter la croix!
Ton histoire est une épopée
Des plus brillants exploits,
God keep our land glorious and free!
O Canada, we stand on guard for thee.
O Canada, we stand on guard for thee.

CHAPTER 6

Making a Living

CANADA HAS ONE OF THE LARGEST AND MOST ROBUST economies in the world. As such, it is one of the world's wealthiest nations. Most Canadians work in service industries, but the nation also has abundant natural resources that contribute much to its economy.

Services

The largest part of Canada's economy is its service sector. Roughly three out of every four working Canadians are employed in service industries. Key areas in this sector include retail sales, health care, communications, education, and entertainment. Tourism is one of the largest service industries. Most foreign visitors to Canada come from the United States and Asia. The development of Canadian casinos has contributed to the increase in tourism, as well as the growth in retail shopping and dining.

In Canada, the basic unit of currency is the dollar, which is divided into one hundred cents. Banknotes come in denominations of $5, $10, $20, $50, and $100. Coins come in values of 1, 5, 10, 25, and 50 cents, as well $1 and $2. Canada's $1 coin is nicknamed the loonie because it has a picture of a common loon on it. Canadian banknotes are more colorful than American bills, with each having a different dominant color. The bills show a notable Canadian figure on the front and a Canadian scene on the back. The $10 bill, for example, depicts Sir John A. Macdonald, Canada's first prime minister, on the front and a passenger train called the Canadian on the back. In 2017, $1.00 Canadian equaled US$0.75, and US$1.00 equaled $1.34 Canadian.

Agriculture

Agriculture has been one of the mainstays of Canada's economy for centuries. Canada is one of the world's leaders in wheat production. It also produces other crops such as soybeans, barley, canola seeds, lentils, and corn.

A percentage of animal-related products from Canada includes those of traditionally domesticated animals such as cows, pigs, and poultry.

Fishing and Forestry

Canada is also rich in natural resources. Almost half the nation is covered in forest, and Canada is one of the world's top producers of timber. In the eastern part of the country, much of the wood is turned into processed wood products such as pulp and paper. In western areas, the timber is more likely to be used for furniture and building materials.

The nation also has rich fishing grounds. Canadians harvest huge amounts of shellfish such as crabs and lobsters. They also catch huge amounts of fish such as haddock, sole, herring, halibut, mackerel, and more. Much of the fish hauled in by Canadian fishers is exported.

A truck filled with logs in southern British Columbia. Quebec, British Columbia, and Ontario are the most active provinces in the forestry industry.

Pumpjacks help bring oil up from beneath the ground of snowy fields in Alberta.

Mining

Mineral resources are a major part of Canada's economy. Canada is a world leader in the production of iron ore, nickel, zinc, copper, gold, silver, platinum, lead, and diamonds. In addition, it produces coal and uranium for the energy market, and gypsum, potash, and limestone, which are used extensively in industrial fabrication.

Canada has also become a key player in the oil market and now places among the top ten oil-producing nations in the world. Much of Canada's oil occurs within sandy deposits, making it more complex and expensive to extract and refine. Canada also has vast natural gas reserves. Like oil, natural gas is used for things such as heating and cooking.

Manufacturing

Manufacturing once played a large role in the Canadian economy. Throughout the twentieth century, once-bustling manufacturing industries began to shrink, with much of the manufacturing being replaced by machines or moved overseas where labor costs less. Even given these changes, Canada's manufacturing has remained a larger part of the national economy than manufacturing is in many other nations, including the United States. Many American companies, in fact, have moved manufacturing plants to Canada. The reasons for this are numerous, including the generally lower cost of labor, Canada's highly educated workforce, and the fact that in Canada health care costs are mostly covered by the government.

Canada manufactures a broad array of products, including chemicals, plastics, rubber, beverages, machinery, computers and other electronics, textiles, transportation equipment, oil, building materials, jewelry, toys, and office supplies. Canada's paper production is among the highest in the world because of its ready supply of timber. Similarly, Canada is a global leader in printed products such as books, magazines, posters, and greeting cards.

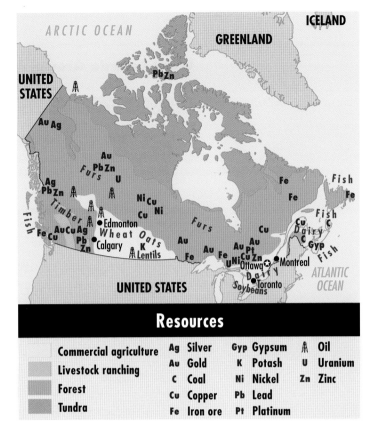

Resources

Commercial agriculture	Ag	Silver	Gyp	Gypsum	A	Oil
Livestock ranching	Au	Gold	K	Potash	U	Uranium
Forest	C	Coal	Ni	Nickel	Zn	Zinc
Tundra	Cu	Copper	Pb	Lead		
	Fe	Iron ore	Pt	Platinum		

What Canada Grows, Makes, and Mines

AGRICULTURE (2015, VALUE OF EXPORTS)

Wheat	US$6.2 billion
Canola seeds	US$4.9 billion
Lentils	US$2.4 billion

MANUFACTURING (2015, VALUE OF EXPORTS)

Vehicles	US$44.9 billion
Machines, engines, and pumps	US$31.1 billion
Electronic equipment	US$13.2 billion

MINING (2015, VALUE OF EXPORTS)

Gold	US$6.9 billion
Diamonds	US$2.6 billion
Silver	US$1.4 billion

Imports and Exports

Trade with other nations is vital to Canada's economy. Canadians export around US$389 billion dollars worth of goods each year and import about US$405 billion. The United States is Canada's biggest trade partner by far. About 75 percent of Canada's exports are sent to the United States, while about 54 percent of the nation's imports come from America. Canada's other leading trade partners include China, Mexico, Japan, and the United Kingdom.

Recent Challenges

Canada has faced a variety of economic challenges in recent years. Although exploiting natural resources has contributed to Canada's prosperity, it can also damage the environment and destroy animal habitats. Although some naturally occurring resources are renewable—trees can be planted and fish can reproduce—some resources are in fact being depleted faster than they can be replenished. Additionally, as nonrenewable resources such as oil and gold become more scarce, companies will want to push into previously undisturbed natural areas in the search for the next great strike.

A fisher off Newfoundland hauls in huge numbers of cod. Fishers once caught so many cod in the North Atlantic that the fish almost disappeared. Today, fisheries are carefully managed.

CHAPTER 7

The Canadian People

CANADIANS HAVE ROOTS ALL OVER THE WORLD. They embody a broad ethnic mix across the country's vast area. To many Canadians, that diversity is central to their national identity. In Canada, people have the right, by law, to express their ethnic identity.

Indigenous People

More than 1.7 million people in Canada identify as indigenous. They fall into three separate groups: The Inuit people live in the arctic regions; First Nations groups live farther south; and the Métis belong to a group that has had mixed indigenous and French traditions since the seventeenth century.

The Inuit people make up the majority of the population in Nunavut and about half the population in the Northwest Territories. They belong to a number of different ethnic groups that speak different dialects of Inuktitut, the Inuit language. In Nunavut, almost all Inuits can still speak Inuktitut. In Canada as a whole, about 64 percent of Inuits can speak their

An Inuit boy sits on a snowmobile. Snowmobiles are one of the most common ways for Inuits to get around in northern Canada.

traditional language, the highest percentage of any indigenous group. Traditionally, the Inuit people lived by hunting and fishing. They ate whales, seals, caribou, ducks, fish, and other creatures. Today, these foods are still important to the Inuit, but they also eat produce, dairy products, and other foods that are shipped north from more southerly regions. Although some Inuits still work as hunters, many others work in mining, the tourist industry, or other jobs.

The First Nations category incorporates a wide range of people. Today, there are 634 First Nations ethnic groups and bands recognized by the Canadian government. Altogether, they speak more than fifty different languages and hundreds of dialects. The largest group is the Cree, which has a population of more than 300,000. They traditionally lived on the plains and across the subarctic regions. Today, more than half of them live on their traditional reserves, while the rest have moved elsewhere. Cultures vary widely among the First

A Cree man takes part in a ceremony in Alberta.

Nations groups. The Crees' traditional nomadic hunting culture is very different from that of the Haidas, the Tsimshians, and other Pacific coast groups, which had ready access to salmon and other foods, leaving them time to develop complex settled cultures. Today, British Columbia has 198 First Nations groups, the largest number of any province.

Métis are people who have a mix of European and indigenous ancestry and identify as Métis. The best-known Métis group emerged along the Red River in Manitoba, merging Cree and French Canadian traditions. Today, Métis culture still

French Canadians take part in a festival celebrating New France in a historic neighborhood in Quebec City.

A Muslim family heads out to dinner in Toronto. Since the 1970s, many Muslims have immigrated to Canada from a variety of nations in Asia and Africa.

shows these influences. Their traditional music incorporates European-style fiddling, and some Métis artwork incorporates European flower designs into traditional indigenous beading. About four hundred thousand Canadians are Métis.

Immigration and Ethnicity

Europeans began settling permanently in Canada in the sixteenth century. First came the French, the English, and the Scottish. By the nineteenth century, Canada was welcoming large numbers of immigrants from other parts of Europe, such as Germany and Italy. In the early twentieth century, Canada enacted laws that limited immigration from Asian countries. Laws favoring European immigrants were changed in the

Ethnic Canada*	
European	76.7%
Asian	14.2%
Indigenous	4.3%
Black	2.9%
Latin American	1.2%
Multiracial	0.5%
Other	0.3%

*Total does not equal 100% because of rounding.

Girls at a Sikh festival in Toronto. Sikhism is a religion that began in India in the 1500s. Today, Canada has the second-highest Sikh population in the world, after India.

1960s, and Canada began welcoming immigrants from all over the world. In the coming decades, people would come from India, China, the Philippines, Pakistan, Iran, and dozens of other nations.

Today, Canada continues to be a country that is welcoming to immigrants. In recent times, about 250,000 immigrants have arrived in Canada each year. Canada is now the site of some of the most diverse cities in the world. Half the people who live in Toronto were born in a foreign country. No one group dominates. Almost half are what the Canadian government terms "visible minorities," which includes people of Asian, African, Middle Eastern, and Latin American descent.

Nearly 13 percent of the people are East Asian, 12 percent are South Asian, 9 percent are black, and another 7 percent are Southeast Asian. Similarly, in Vancouver, British Columbia, just over half the people are visible minorities, and people of East and Southeast Asian descent are the most common. They make up 40 percent of the total population.

Women snowboard on a mountain in British Columbia. A quarter of the people in British Columbia are "visible minorities," the highest percentage of any province.

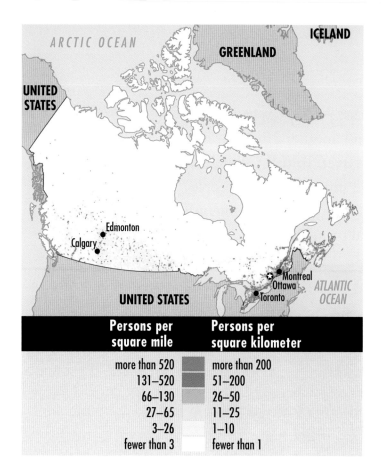

Persons per square mile		Persons per square kilometer	
more than 520		more than 200	
131–520		51–200	
66–130		26–50	
27–65		11–25	
3–26		1–10	
fewer than 3		fewer than 1	

Population of Largest Cities (2016 est.)

Toronto, Ontario	2,731,571
Montreal, Quebec	1,704,694
Calgary, Alberta	1,239,220
Ottawa, Ontario	934,243
Edmonton, Alberta	932,546

Population

When the Dominion of Canada was formed in 1867, the country had a population of about 3.5 million. Today, the country is home to more than ten times as many people—more than 36 million in 2016.

Canada is a vast country, but much of it has few people. About 82 percent of the population lives in urban areas. And most people are concentrated into the more southerly parts of the country, even if they live in small towns or in the countryside. The province of Ontario, for example, is home to just under 40 percent of Canada's population, whereas the Northwest Territories, Nunavut, Prince Edward Island, and the Yukon don't even have 1 percent combined. And members of some ethnic groups are concentrated in certain areas. Most Inuits, for example, live in Nunavut, while most people of French ancestry are found in the province of Quebec.

Language

Canada has two official languages: English and French. English is the official language in most of the provinces. French, however, is the official language in Quebec, and New Brunswick

A sign welcomes visitors in English, French, and two versions of Inuktitut, an Inuit language.

is bilingual. About three out of five Canadians speak English at home, while one out of five speaks French.

Other common languages spoken in Canada include Mandarin Chinese, Punjabi (from India), Cantonese Chinese, Italian, Spanish, Tagalog (from the Philippines), and Arabic. Many indigenous languages are also spoken in Canada. In Nunavut, for example, the Inuit people speak languages such as Inuktitut and Inuinnaqtun. In the Northwest Territories, languages such as Chipewyan, Cree, and Slavey are common.

French Phrase	Pronunciation	English Translation
Bonjour	bohn-zhoor	Hello
Je m'appelle...	zhuh mah-pehl	My name is...
S'il vous plaît	seel voo pleh	Please
Merci	mehr-see	Thank you
De rien	dah ree-ehn	You're welcome
Au revoir	o ruh-vwahr	Good-bye
Excusez-moi	ehk-kew-zay mwah	Excuse me
Je t'aime	zhuh-tehm	I love you
Je voudrais...	zhuh voo-dreh	I would like...

Education

Children in Canada begin school between ages four and seven, depending on which province they live in.

The education system in Canada is similar to that in the United States. In Canada, the school year starts in late August and runs until around the end of June. In both countries,

education is divided into three large sections, primary (elementary school), secondary (high school), and post-secondary (college). In Canada, children start primary school at age five or six. They learn subjects such as math, science, literature, and history. Many Canadian schoolchildren learn both English and French. In many Quebec schools, all classes are taught in French.

The majority of Canadians—about 70 percent—continue with some sort of education after high school. This makes Canadians among the most educated people in the world. The nation's largest university is the University of Toronto, which serves more than seventy thousand students. Other large Canadian universities include York University, which is also in Toronto, the University of British Columbia, and the University of Alberta. In Montreal, the University of Montreal offers classes in French, while McGill University is a highly regarded English-language school.

Students relax at the University of Toronto. Two out of three Canadians have a degree from a college or vocational school.

CHAPTER 8

Spiritual Life

IN CANADA'S EARLIEST DAYS, INDIGENOUS PEOPLES practiced religions that were closely connected to the natural world. There was a wide range of beliefs and practices, but often indigenous peoples believed that all things found in nature, such as animals and plants, possessed a spirit, and that these spirits could influence the human world. For example, the Netsilik Inuit believed in a spirit named Nuliajuk, who made it impossible to catch fish when she was angered. Another spirit, Sila, had powerful influence over the weather.

In many of the indigenous cultures of Canada, religious leaders, sometimes called shamans, were believed to be able to contact the spirit world. Communication with the spirits was believed to be able to help humans in many different ways. The spirits might help people find food when it became scarce, or keep them safe from harsh weather. Communication with the spirits might also help heal the sick.

Opposite: **Catholics in Montreal take part in a procession on Easter. Quebec has the highest proportion of Catholics of any province.**

Some members of Canada's First Nations, Inuit, and Métis communities continue to practice their traditional religions.

The Arrival of Christianity

Europeans brought Christianity to Canada's shores. The earliest French settlers, who began arriving in large numbers in the early 1600s, brought their beliefs along with their clothes, books, and other valuables. These early French settlers were Catholic, and they believed it was important to spread their faith to the indigenous peoples they encountered. Some of the people already living in Canada resisted these teachings, while others embraced it. In some cases, the traditional religion and Catholicism merged. In other cases, traditional beliefs were abandoned altogether.

By the eighteenth century, settlers from other European nations, such as England, Holland, Germany, and Switzerland, had arrived.

A figure used by Inuit shamans to represent spirits.

Turtle Island

People the world over have told stories to explain how the world came into being. Several First Nations groups tell the story about a turtle and a muskrat. According to this creation story, the earth was once completely covered with water. The muskrat dove to the bottom of the ocean to bring dirt to the surface so a landmass could be created. To do this, the muskrat had to pile the dirt on the back of a turtle. In time, the land grew large enough to live on. Even today, some indigenous Canadians refer to North America as Turtle Island.

Most were not Catholic. Instead, they practiced different forms of Protestant Christianity, including Episcopalianism, Lutheranism, Methodism, and Presbyterianism. Many of these Protestant settlers also tried to spread their beliefs to the indigenous people of Canada. These religious differences contributed to the tensions that evolved between the French and other European settlers in the years ahead.

A French missionary rides in a canoe with Native Americans. Some of the first French people in Canada were missionaries.

Catholics attend Mass at a church in Quebec City.

Religion Today

Today, Christianity remains the leading religion in Canada. Nearly four out of ten Canadians are Catholic and nearly three out of ten are Protestant or Orthodox Christian. For most Christian Canadians, attending church services is not a regular part of their lives. Attendance of worship services has steadily declined in recent years. Newfoundland and

Labrador has the largest percentage Christian population. About 94 percent of the people there identify as Christian. British Columbia has the least amount of people who identify as Christian, about 45 percent.

Although Christianity is the most widespread faith in Canada, the Canada government does not recognize an official religion. Instead, the government encourages religious freedom, meaning Canadians are welcome to worship in whatever way they want. Today, Canadians belong to many different religions.

Muslim women praying in Ottawa. Muslims pray five times a day.

The second most common religion in the country is Islam. About 3 percent of the population is Muslim. The first mosque in Canada was built in Edmonton in 1938. The largest numbers of Canadian Muslims live near Toronto and Montreal. Many have Indian, Pakistani, and Iranian ancestry. The number of Muslims in Canada is expected to continue to increase as Canada welcomes many Muslim immigrants.

Women carry offerings during a Hindu festival in Montreal.

Roughly 2 percent of Canadians are Hindu. Most Canadian Hindus trace their ancestry to India or Sri Lanka. Ontario is home to the most Hindus in Canada, but British Columbia and Quebec also have large populations. Canadian Sikhs also have their origins in India. Their largest numbers are in British Columbia.

About 1 percent of Canadians are Jewish. Large numbers of Jewish people left Russia and other parts of eastern Europe and migrated to Canada in late 1800s and early 1900s. Today, Montreal and Toronto are home to the largest Jewish communities in the nation.

Nearly a quarter of the Canadian population does not belong to any religion at all. As with so many other subjects, Canadians consider religion a personal matter and generally keep their religious views to themselves.

Montreal has a large Jewish population, including a community of ultra-Orthodox Hasidim, who dress in dark, formal clothes.

Religion in Canada*

Roman Catholic	38.7%
Other Christian	28.5%
Muslim	3.2%
Hindu	1.5%
Sikh	1.4%
Buddhist	1.1%
Jewish	1.0%
Other	0.6%
Nonreligious	23.9%

*Total does not equal 100% because of rounding.

CHAPTER 9

Arts and Sports

CANADIANS, LIKE PEOPLE ALL OVER THE WORLD, express who they are through the literature they create. Canadian writers have infused much of their output with wry humor. Many explore the immigrant experience and the search for identity. They frequently address serious issues using humor and subtlety rather than using a more direct approach.

Canada has produced many fine authors, some of whom have attained international success. In 2013, Alice Munro won the Nobel Prize in Literature, the world's top literary award, for her subtle short stories.

Another widely recognized Canadian author is Margaret Atwood. Born in Ontario in 1939, Atwood is a novelist, poet, essayist, and critic. Her writing delves into questions about the status of women in society, environmental issues, and the

Opposite: **An Inuit carving from the Northwest Territories**

question of Canada's cultural identity. Her books include *The Blind Assassin*, winner of the prestigious Man Booker Prize given annually to the best novel published in English.

Children's author L. M. Montgomery was born on Prince Edward Island in 1874. Montgomery lived with her grandparents after the death of her mother and became something of a loner. From this loneliness came a sharp and vivid imagination, which helped her develop the beloved Anne of Green Gables series about a spirited orphan girl who moves in with an elderly couple.

Alice Munro was the first Canadian to win the Nobel Prize in Literature.

Music

Canada has a robust music scene, covering a variety of styles. The nation's huge musical output is helped by a government that has enthusiastically supported its musical talent and is willing to provide financial help to some artists and institutions. Canadian artists have sometimes felt overwhelmed by the amount of music produced in the United States. In response to the American dominance of popular culture, Canada passed a law in the late 1960s requiring that a certain amount of the music played on the radio be by Canadian artists. Similarly, a certain percentage of the TV shows broadcast in Canada have to be Canadian.

The earliest forms of Canadian music came from the First Nations and Inuit people. Since there were so many distinct

Canadians film a TV show in Ottawa. Sixty percent of the programming on broadcast television in Canada must be of Canadian origin.

A Celtic fiddler from Nova Scotia. Fiddlers from this region are known for playing with a driving energy.

populations and communities, there were many different musical forms. People fashioned instruments out of whatever materials were available to them, including animal skins and bones, wood, and rocks. Music was central to storytelling and religious rituals. It was often accompanied by dancing or chanting.

Europeans brought other kinds of music to Canada. These included classical music and folk music from a variety of cultures. Celtic music, for example, came to Nova Scotia with Scottish immigrants. To this day, the region still has a strong traditional Celtic music scene featuring fantastic fiddlers. In the mid-twentieth century, Canadian music was broadened by people originating from other cultures who immigrated to Canada. The music of the United States was also having a powerful effect, and many Canadians took up jazz, country, and rock and roll.

Canadians have excelled in every genre of music. Glenn Gould, one of the greatest classical music pianists of all time, was from Toronto. Oscar Peterson and Maynard Ferguson brought jazz to new heights, and Hank Snow was inducted into the Country Music Hall of Fame. The number of pop and rock artists from Canada who have gone on to international

Oscar Peterson (sitting) is considered one of the greatest pianists in the history of jazz. He had a style that was both relaxed and ornate.

Funny Folk

Many of the most successful comedy performers in American TV and film are in fact Canadian. Lorne Michaels, who created *Saturday Night Live* (*SNL*) in 1975, grew up in Toronto. Many *SNL* cast members over the years have been Canadian, including Dan Aykroyd, John Candy, Martin Short, and Mike Myers. Other Canadian comedians, such as Jim Carrey, have made their name in films. Carrey is known for slapstick humor, as in *Dumb and Dumber*, but he has also made more serious movies, such as *The Truman Show*.

fame is staggering, and encompasses such greats as 1960s and 1970s legends Neil Young and Rush as well as modern favorites Avril Lavigne, Céline Dion, Shania Twain, Drake, Justin Bieber, and Michael Bublé.

Justin Bieber became a pop star while still a teenager.

The National Gallery of Canada

One of the most popular destinations in Canada for visitors and residents alike is the National Gallery of Canada. Located in the capital city of Ottawa, its current building opened in 1988. The museum features a stunning array of drawings, sculpture, paintings, photography, and other arts. The pride of the National Gallery is known as the Canadian Collection, which features works from the nation's most important artists such as Tom Thomson, Emily Carr, and Jean-Paul Riopelle. The museum also features works by top artists from around the world, including Vincent van Gogh, Claude Monet, and Andy Warhol. Outside the museum stands a huge sculpture of a spider by Louise Bourgeois.

Visual Arts

Canada's contributions to the visual arts also date back to First Nations and Inuit people, who created drawings and ornate carvings, often depicting animal figures. Many of these artworks were used in ceremonies, along with dance and music. The arrival of Europeans introduced different materials and subject matter. By the mid-1800s, many Canadian artists were depicting the landscape and people around them. Part of the driving force behind the sudden popularity of landscape paintings was the need for European governments to record and illustrate these regions that were new to them. Portraiture, meanwhile, had been popular in Europe for decades before it caught on among Canadian artists.

The beginning of the twentieth century saw a new approach in Canadian visual arts. There was a vigorous

Autumn Hillside, by Franklin Carmichael, one of the Group of Seven

attempt to illustrate some form of national identity. Among those who led this effort was the Group of Seven, made up of seven of the most accomplished landscape painters of the time. These artists decided that the essence of the Canadian character could best be found in Canada's vast and varied natural surroundings. They traveled together in search of the scenery that seemed to best characterize the young nation, and painted it. Their efforts were widely influential and eventually evolved into the Canadian Group of Painters, which continued to influence future generations of artists.

Sports

Canadians love sports, in both summer and winter. Popular sports in Canada best done during warm times of the year include golf, volleyball, tennis, basketball, baseball, football, soccer, rugby, swimming, and cycling. Canada has produced professional athletes in all these sports, and they compete at an international level.

Many Canadians bicycle year-round, even in the snow.

In winter, Canadians enjoy sports such as skating and skiing. By far, the most popular sport in Canada is hockey. Hockey has existed in its present form since the late 1800s and is integrated into just about all aspects of Canadian life. There are professional leagues for both men and women, as well as amateur leagues for children. Some of the best players in hockey history have been Canadian, including

Backcountry skiing is growing in popularity. Some skiers are even dropped on mountaintops by helicopter, so they can ski through the pristine wilderness.

The Great One

Many people consider Wayne Gretzky to be the greatest hockey player of all time. Gretzky was born in Brantford, Ontario, in 1961. He began skating a few years after he learned to walk, and he was so enthusiastic that his parents provided him with his own skating rink on their family farm. It wasn't long before he was playing with boys much older than he was and piling up incredible statistics. In one early league, he stunned locals by scoring more than five hundred points (the combined total of goals and assists) in a single season.

In 1978, at age seventeen, Gretzky signed his first professional contract, with a team in the World Hockey Association called the Indianapolis Racers. Later that same year, he joined the Edmonton Oilers in the National Hockey League (NHL). This was where he would make his mark on history. In his rookie year, he won the NHL's Most Valuable Player award. In the years that followed, he broke record after record, including one that has stood for thirty-five years—scoring at least one goal in over fifty consecutive games. He is also the only player to score more than two hundred points in a single season—a feat he accomplished on four separate occasions. A third remarkable accomplishment was his scoring four goals in a single period—just twenty minutes of play.

By the time Gretzky retired in 1999 after a career of superhuman proportion, he was known as the Great One, and the NHL permanently retired his jersey number, 99, throughout the entire league.

Canada's women's hockey team defeated the United States in 2014 to win Olympic gold.

Wayne Gretzky and Gordie Howe. Canada's national women's hockey team is tremendously accomplished. It has won the gold medal in the Olympic Winter Games four times. It has also won more than ten World Championships and more than a dozen Nations Cups.

Canada has two national sports. The national winter sport is hockey, and the national summer sport is lacrosse, although lacrosse is played year-round. An early form of lacrosse was played by indigenous people in the region as far back as the 1500s. In Canada, there are both men's and women's lacrosse

Brooms on the Ice

Canada is the world leader in the unusual sport called curling. Invented in Scotland in the 1500s, curling involves sliding stones on the ice toward a target. The players sweep the ice in front of the stone to reduce friction, so the stone will travel farther and end up exactly where they want it to. Canadians have won more medals in Olympic curling than players from any other nation.

leagues, and Canadian teams have won many international competitions, including the 2006 World Championship, held in Ontario.

Canada has one of the world's top lacrosse teams.

CHAPTER 10

Everyday Life

CANADIANS HAVE A REPUTATION FOR BEING POLITE and friendly. Many visitors to Canada comment on how nice the average Canadian is. In Canada, a high value is placed on respect and civility.

Canadians tend to be informal, at home and at work. It is common for them to prefer to be called by their first names, and people generally act and speak in a relaxed manner. Canadians also make a point of being easily accessible and approachable. The culture tends toward modesty, as many wealthy Canadians avoid flaunting their money. Their attitude is that no one should ever develop too lofty an image of themselves!

Opposite: **Most families in Canada have either one or two children.**

Many Canadians have a do-everything-early attitude toward their daily routine. Many are early risers, early workers, and even early eaters. Breakfast is sometimes served well before the sun comes up, lunch an hour before noon, and dinner is scheduled for five o'clock. Some Canadians go to bed early as well.

While outwardly friendly, Canadians also have a reputation of being somewhat reserved. They tend to keep personal matters to themselves. For example, they often do not talk about their health issues or political views. Most Canadians keep their opinions private and do not ask for other people's opinions. These beliefs have produced a society where most people are polite in public and cordial and agreeable to strangers.

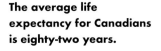

The average life expectancy for Canadians is eighty-two years.

A Canadian woman enjoys time with her granddaughter.

Family Customs

Canadian weddings are much the same as American weddings. If a couple is Christian, they are usually married in a church with friends and family in attendance. Following the ceremony is a celebratory dinner known as a reception. Then many couples travel to a far-off destination for their honeymoon.

Some wedding traditions are different from American customs, however. One that is becoming less common is the trousseau tea. This is a party hosted by the bride's mother for people who are not invited to the actual wedding.

Many condos have been built in recent years. Young people often live in condos rather than houses, in part because condos are less expensive.

In some parts of Canada there is a tradition called the wedding wheel. In this practice, two lines of guests pay a small amount of money for the privilege of dancing with the bride or groom. The money is then used to help the couple pay for the honeymoon or for goods they need for their home. A variation on this is a shoe dance, in which the bride dances barefoot with people while holding one of her shoes, which is then filled with money.

Traditions at the end of life are also similar to those in the United States. Christian funerals often involve three parts: the viewing, where the deceased is laid in the coffin and guests come to pay their respects; the service, where a minister leads a service in a church; and the burial, where the deceased is placed in the ground in a cemetery. There are many variations in funerals. Some people prefer to have the body cremated, and the ashes are often given to the family of the deceased. People of Irish heritage sometimes throw lavish parties called wakes. The purpose of these is to focus on the positive aspects of the deceased's life. Similarly, many church funerals now include popular music that helps create an uplifting atmosphere that focuses on the deceased's life rather than the fact that he or she has passed on.

Canadians drop red poppies on the Tomb of the Unknown Soldier in Ottawa. In Canada, poppies are a traditional remembrance for soldiers who have died.

Fill It Up

A popular game among Canadian children is known as Fill It Up. It requires lots of water and can get quite messy, so it needs to be played outdoors. To play, it is necessary to have:

- Four buckets—two for each team
- Small plastic cups for each player
- A measuring cup to determine the winner

The game is played as follows:

1. Split the children into two teams.
2. Fill one of each team's buckets with water.
3. Place the empty bucket across a field from the full bucket.
4. Line up the two teams in a single file behind the full bucket, and have them take turns putting water into their cup and transferring it to their empty bucket. It's okay if they put their hand over the top as they go along in order to avoid spilling.
5. The game ends when all the water is taken from the first bucket and emptied into the second bucket.
6. Using the measuring cup, measure the water in each bucket. The team with the most water wins.

Let's Eat

As diverse as Canada's population is, so is the food the country enjoys. A single street might have a fast-food hamburger restaurant next to a Moroccan restaurant next to a Japanese restaurant. Naturally, areas that are home to many people with the same ethnic background have a large number of restaurants with that kind of food. For example, Quebec has more French restaurants than other parts of the country.

Maple syrup is sometimes sold in decorative bottles shaped like maple leaves.

One food item that is closely associated with Canada is maple syrup. Canada produces about 80 percent of the world's maple syrup. Most of it is produced in Quebec. Canadian maple syrup has a remarkably rich flavor, which many people say is different from maple syrup made in other countries. In Canada, maple syrup is not only eaten on pancakes and waffles. It is put on sausages, fruit, or ice cream; used as a sweetener in drinks; and used in baked goods to add flavor and sweetness.

Another food associated with Canada is called poutine. It is a filling snack food that is believed to have originated in Quebec. Poutine consists of French fries topped with cheese curds and brown gravy. Some restaurants offer variations on poutine, topping it with meat or cabbage.

No one is sure who first made poutine, but it likely got its start in Quebec in the 1950s.

Spicy Ketchup Seasoning

A popular snack item in Canada is called ketchup chips. These are potato chips covered in a spicy, ketchup-based seasoning. The ketchup seasoning is also delicious on popcorn. Have an adult help you with this recipe.

Ingredients

12 cups air-popped popcorn (about $1/3$ cup kernels)

2 tablespoons butter

2 tablespoons sugar

2 tablespoons tomato paste

4 teaspoons white vinegar

$1/2$ teaspoon smoked paprika

$1/2$ teaspoon salt

$1/4$ teaspoon onion powder

$1/4$ teaspoon garlic powder

Directions

1. Preheat the oven to 300°F.
2. Pop the popcorn according to the instructions on the package.
3. Melt the butter over medium heat in a small saucepan. Whisk in the sugar, tomato paste, vinegar, smoked paprika, salt, onion powder, and garlic powder. Stir constantly until the sugar is dissolved. This should take about 1 minute.
4. In a large bowl, toss the popcorn with the tomato mixture in order to coat it. Then spread the coated popcorn on a large baking sheet.
5. Bake in the oven, stirring once after a few minutes, until the coating is dry to the touch, after about 15 to 18 minutes. Let the popcorn cool on the pan for 10 minutes.
6. Enjoy!

Members of a marching band wear Canada's red and white colors for a Canada Day parade in Alberta.

Holidays

Canada has just five holidays that are recognized across the nation—New Year's Day, Good Friday, Canada Day, Labour Day, and Christmas. Canadians celebrate many other official holidays, but they are determined by the provincial government rather than the national government. This is one of the ways in which Canada's provinces have more independence from the federal government than the U.S. states do.

National Holidays

New Year's Day	January 1
Good Friday	March or April
Canada Day	July 1
Labour Day	September
Christmas	December 25

One of Canada's provincial holidays is Family Day, which encourages parents to take the day off and spend time with their families—not just their children, but other relatives as

Shoppers stroll through Old Quebec City during the Christmas season.

well, such as aunts, uncles, nieces, and nephews. In British Columbia, it is observed on the second Monday in February. In Alberta, Ontario, and Saskatchewan, it is celebrated on the third Monday of February. This holiday is observed in other provinces under different names. In Manitoba it is called Louis Riel Day, on Prince Edward Island it is Islander Day, and in Nova Scotia it is Heritage Day.

Family Day is a time for relaxation and fun.

Fashion

Canadians dress similarly to their neighbors to the south. They wear jeans, T-shirts, and sweaters. Because it is cold for much of the year, warm coats and boots are important.

Canadians are also known for being casual. Many people wear jeans and sneakers to the office. Many Canadian men wear suits only when it is absolutely necessary. Otherwise, they would much rather wear whatever is most practical and comfortable, so they can relax and enjoy life.

Many Canadians enjoy spending time in nature, so outdoor clothes are part of their wardrobe.

Timeline

CANADIAN HISTORY

The fur trade begins to decline.	**1830s**
Nova Scotia, New Brunswick, Ontario, and Quebec unite to create the Dominion of Canada.	**1867**
Miners flood into the Yukon during the Klondike Gold Rush.	**1890s**
Canada joins World War I on the side of the Allies.	**1914**
Canada enters World War II with a declaration of war on Germany.	**1939**
Canada adopts its current maple leaf flag.	**1965**
Pierre Trudeau becomes prime minister.	**1968**
The Official Languages Act gives French and English equal status.	**1969**
Violence erupts over the issue of Quebecois separation from the rest of Canada.	**1970**
Canada becomes fully independent; Canada passes the Canadian Charter of Rights and Freedoms.	**1982**
Canada, the United States, and Mexico sign the North American Free Trade Agreement.	**1994**
Nunavut becomes a territory, the first with a largely indigenous population.	**1999**
Canada becomes the first nation in the Americas to legalize same-sex marriage.	**2005**
Justin Trudeau becomes prime minister.	**2015**

WORLD HISTORY

1865	The American Civil War ends.
1879	The first practical lightbulb is invented.
1914	World War I begins.
1917	The Bolshevik Revolution brings communism to Russia.
1929	A worldwide economic depression begins.
1939	World War II begins.
1945	World War II ends.
1969	Humans land on the Moon.
1975	The Vietnam War ends.
1989	The Berlin Wall is torn down as communism crumbles in Eastern Europe.
1991	The Soviet Union breaks into separate states.
2001	Terrorists attack the World Trade Center in New York City and the Pentagon near Washington, D.C.
2004	A tsunami in the Indian Ocean destroys coastlines in Africa, India, and Southeast Asia.
2008	The United States elects its first African American president.
2016	Donald Trump is elected U.S. president.

Fast Facts

Official name: Canada

Capital: Ottawa

Official languages: English and French

Montreal

National flag

Official religion: None

National anthem: "O Canada"

Type of government: Constitutional monarchy

Head of state: Monarch of the United Kingdom

Head of government: Prime Minister

Area of country: 3,855,103 square miles (9,984,670 sq km)

Bordering country: United States to the south and west

Highest elevation: Mount Logan, 19,551 feet (5,959 m) above sea level

Lowest elevation: Sea level along the coast

Longest river: Mackenzie River, 2,635 miles (4,241 km)

Largest lake: Lake Superior, 31,700 square miles (82,100 sq km)

Highest recorded temperature: 113°F (45°C), in Yellow Grass and Midale, Saskatchewan, on July 5, 1937

Lowest recorded temperature: −81.4°F (−63°C), in Snag, Yukon, on February 3, 1947

Mount Logan

CN Tower

Currency

National population (2016 est.): 36,443,632

Population of largest cities (2016 est.):

Toronto, Ontario	2,731,571
Montreal, Quebec	1,704,694
Calgary, Alberta	1,239,220
Ottawa, Ontario	934,243
Edmonton, Alberta	932,546

Landmarks:
- ▶ *Banff National Park,* Alberta
- ▶ *CN Tower,* Toronto
- ▶ *National Gallery of Canada,* Ottawa
- ▶ *Old Quebec,* Quebec City
- ▶ *Pacific Rim National Park Reserve,* British Columbia

Economy: Most Canadians work in service industries. Tourism is a growing industry. Canada is a major supplier of oil and natural gas. Many resources are mined there, including iron ore, nickel, zinc, gold, silver, and diamonds. Other valuable natural resources from Canada are fish and timber. The nation's major manufactured products include transportation equipment, electronics, chemicals, food products, and wood and paper products. Wheat is its most valuable agricultural product.

Currency: Canadian dollar. In 2017, $1.00 Canadian equaled US$0.75, and US$1.00 equaled $1.34 Canadian.

System of weights and measures: Metric system

Literacy rate: 99%

Schoolchildren

Justin Bieber

Common French words and phrases:

Bonjour	Hello
Je m'appelle…	My name is...
Merci	Thank you
De rien	You're welcome
Au revoir	Good-bye
Excusez-moi	Excuse me

Prominent Canadians:

Justin Bieber *Singer*	(1994–)
Samuel de Champlain *Explorer*	(1574–1635)
Wayne Gretzky *Hockey player*	(1961–)
Sir John A. Macdonald *Prime minister*	(1815–1891)
L. M. Montgomery *Novelist*	(1874–1942)
Alice Munro *Nobel Prize–winning writer*	(1931–)
Oscar Peterson *Jazz musician*	(1925–2007)
Pierre Trudeau *Prime minister*	(1919–2000)

To Find Out More

Books

- ▶ Berton, Pierre. *The Klondike Fever: The Life and Death of the Last Great Gold Rush*. New York: Basic Books, 2003.

- ▶ Herman, Gail. *Who Is Wayne Gretzky?* New York: Grosset & Dunlap, 2015.

- ▶ Kallen, Stuart A. *Native Peoples of the Arctic*. Lerner Publications, Minneapolis, MN: 2016.

- ▶ Montgomery, L. M. *Anne of Green Gables*. New York: Aladdin, 2014.

Music

- ▶ *Canada: Inuit Games and Songs*. Washington, DC: Smithsonian Folkways, 2014.

- ▶ *The Heart of Cape Breton*. Washington, DC: Smithsonian Folkways, 2002.

- ▶ *The Rough Guide to the Music of Canada*. London: World Music Network, 2003.

▶ Visit this Scholastic website for more information on Canada:
www.factsfornow.scholastic.com
Enter the keyword **Canada**

Index

Page numbers in *italics*
indicate illustrations.

Meet the Author

WIL MARA IS PART CANADIAN BY ANCESTRY, his paternal grandfather having grown up in the Toronto area before moving to the United States. Mara is also the award-winning author of more than two hundred books, many of them educational titles for children in Scholastic's catalog. He began writing in the late 1980s with several nonfiction titles about herpetology, the study of reptiles and amphibians. He branched out into fiction in the 1990s, when he ghostwrote five of the popular Boxcar Children Mysteries. He has since authored more than a dozen novels, including *Wave*, which was the recipient of the 2005 New Jersey Notable Book Award; *The Gemini Virus*; and *Frame 232*, a *New York Times* bestseller, which reached the number one spot in its category on Amazon.com and won the 2013 Lime Award for Excellence in Fiction.

Photo Credits